Simply Roc

MW00450768

16 Rockin' Hits of the 1990s

Arranged by Dan Coates

Simply Rock 90s is a collection of some of the greatest songs from a pivotal decade in music. These selections have been carefully arranged by Dan Coates for Easy Piano, making them accessible to pianists of all ages. Phrase markings, articulations, fingering, pedaling, and dynamics have been included to aid with interpretation, and a large print size makes the notation easy to read.

As a reaction to the big hair, glamour, and "synthesizer heaven" of the '80s, '90s rock artists turned introspective. Audiences approved, and grunge, indie, and alternative rock dominated mainstream radio and music videos. R.E.M. produced some of the best-selling records. *Out of Time* (1991), the band's seventh album, sold over 10 million copies, and its single "Losing My Religion" won two Grammy awards. Across the Atlantic, alternative rock thrived as well. Radiohead recorded critically and commercially successful albums. "Fake Plastic Trees" (*The Bends*, 1995) showcased lead singer Thom Yorke's falsetto crooning and world-weary lyrics. Other artists also commented on the problems in the world. Van Halen's 1991 hit "Right Now" won MTV's Video of the Year, addressing issues ranging from unfair minimum wage to racism.

Lighter songs also peppered the '90s airwaves. The Rembrandts recorded the catchy "I'll Be There for You" for the hit sitcom *Friends*, which debuted in 1994 and entertained audiences with stories of young, urban life. The 1998 blockbuster film *Armaggedon* featured Aerosmith's power ballad "I Don't Want to Miss a Thing." Mike Myers's flamboyant character Austin Powers inspired "Beautiful Stranger," Madonna's groovy dance-pop song.

Playing the diverse rock music of the '90s on the piano can rekindle fond memories of favorite movies, videos, and albums. Additionally, the familiar rhythms and unforgettable melodies can be learned easily. For these reasons and more, the hits on the following pages are exciting to explore.

After all, this is *Simply Rock 90s*!

Cover illustration by Sarah Vaughan

Contents

Bitter Sweet Symphony

Written by Mick Jagger and Keith Richards
Lyrics by Richard Ashcroft
Arranged by Dan Coates

Verse 2:
Well, I've never prayed,
But tonight I'm on my knees, yeah.
I need to hear some sounds
That recognize the pain in me, yeah.
I let the melody shine,
Let it cleanse my mind.
I feel free now.
But the airwaves are clean
And there's nobody singing to me now.
(To Chorus:)

Verse 3:
'Cause it's a bittersweet symphony, this life.
Tryin' to make ends meet,
Try to find somebody,
Then you die.
I'll take you down the only
Road I've ever been down.
You know, the one that takes you
To the places where all the veins meet, yeah.
(To Chorus:)

Beautiful Stranger

Words and Music by
Madonna and William Orbit
Arranged by Dan Coates

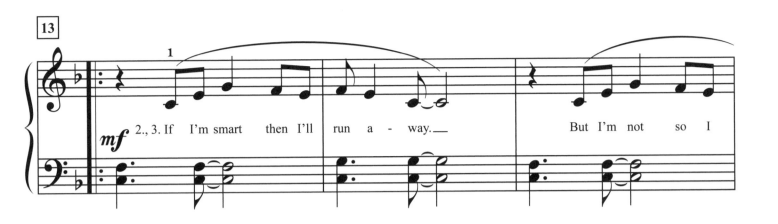

Bridge:

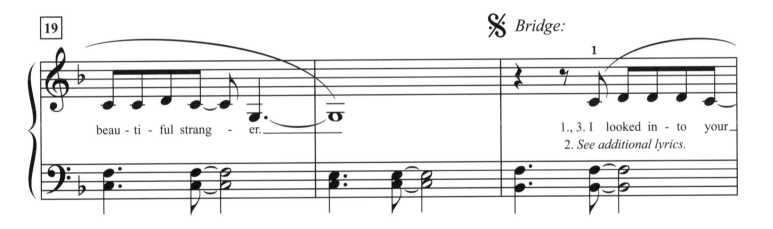

You're the dev - il in dis - guise. That's why I'm sing - ing this song.

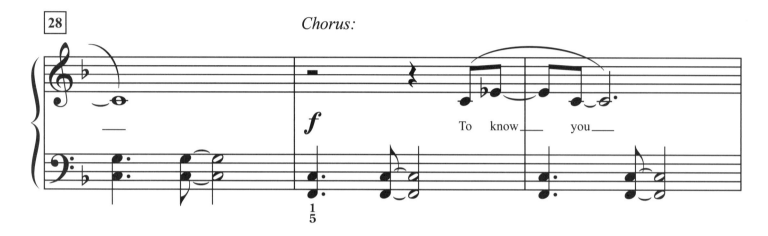

Chorus:

To know you

is to love you. You're ev - 'ry-where I

to Coda ⊕ | 1.

go. And ev - 'ry-bod - y knows.

To love___ you___ is to be part of___

___ you.___ I've paid for you with___ tears___

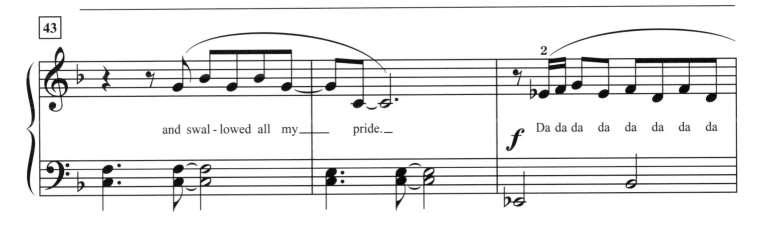

and swal-lowed all my___ pride.___ Da da da da da da da da

da da da da da. Beau-ti-ful strang-er.___

Da da da da da da da da da da da da da. Beau - ti - ful

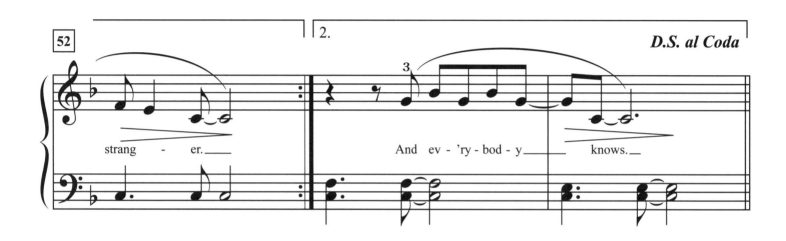

D.S. al Coda

strang - er. And ev - 'ry - bod - y knows.

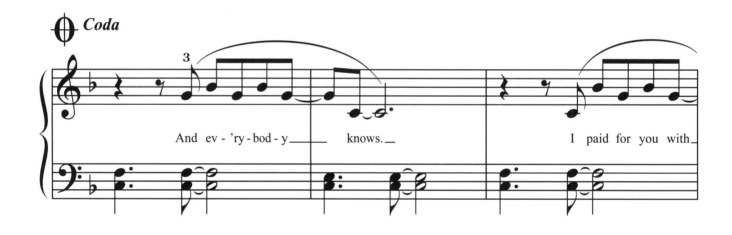

Coda

And ev - 'ry - bod - y knows. I paid for you with

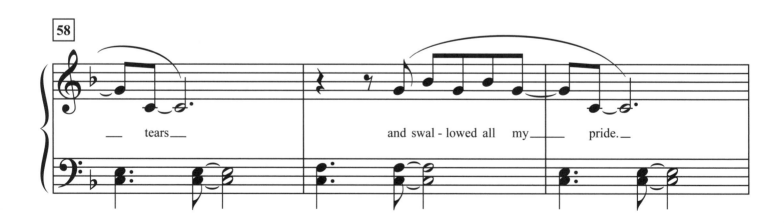

tears and swal - lowed all my pride.

Bridge 2:
I looked into your face,
My heart was dancin' all over the place.
I'd like to change my point of view,
If I could just forget about you.
(To Chorus:)

Breakfast at Tiffany's

Words and Music by Todd Pipes
Arranged by Dan Coates

Moderately, with a steady rock beat

1. You'll say

2., 3. *See additional lyrics.*

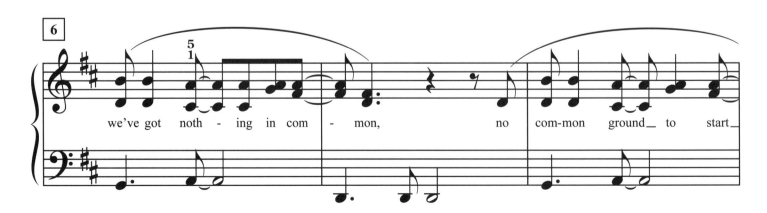

we've got noth - ing in com - mon,   no com-mon ground_ to start

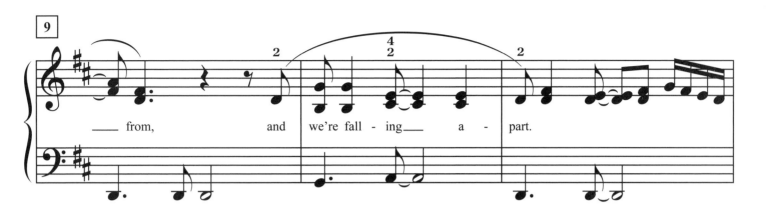

_____ from,   and   we're fall - ing_____ a - part.

You'll say_____   the world has come_ be - tween_

_____ us,   our lives have come_ be - tween_____ us,   still

I know you_____ just don't care.   And I_____

cresc.

Verse 2:
I see you, the only one who knew me,
But now your eyes see through me.
I guess I was wrong.
So what now?
It's plain to see we're over,
I hate when things are over,
When so much is left undone.
(To Chorus:)

Verse 3:
You'll say we've got nothing in common,
No common ground to start from,
And we're falling apart.
You'll say
The world has come between us,
Our lives have come between us,
Still I know you just don't care.
(To Chorus:)

Fake Plastic Trees

Words and Music by
Thomas Yorke, Edward O'Brien, Colin Greenwood,
Jonathan Greenwood and Philip Selway
Arranged by Dan Coates

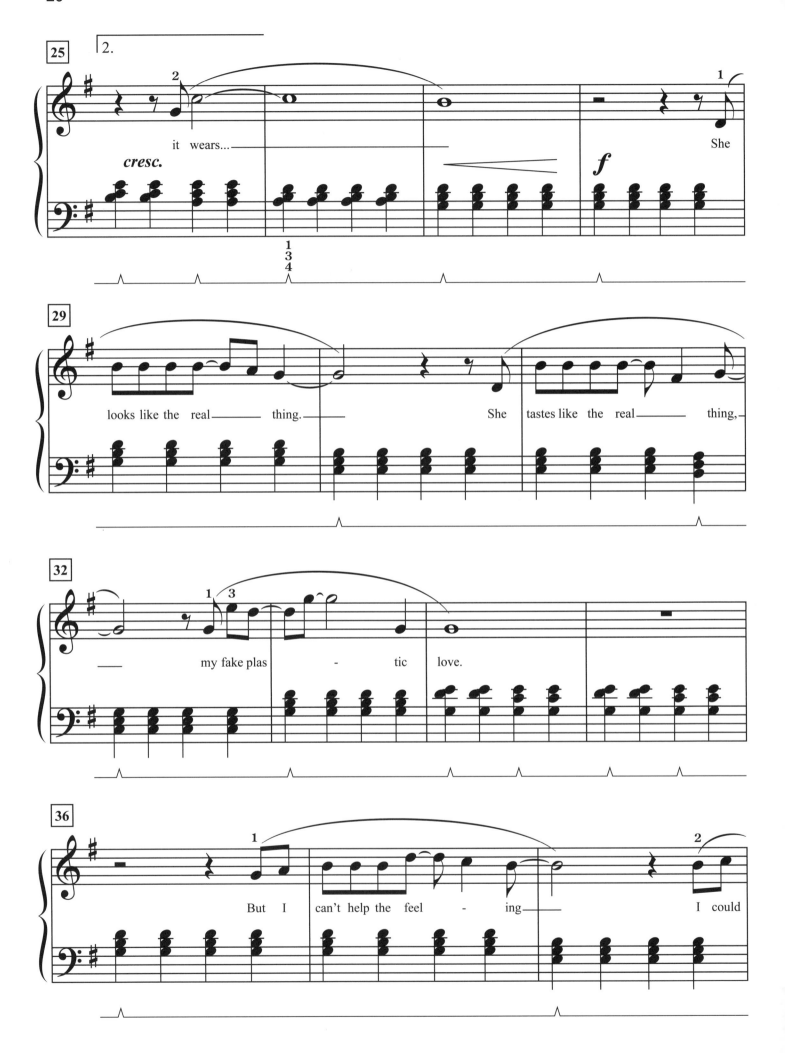

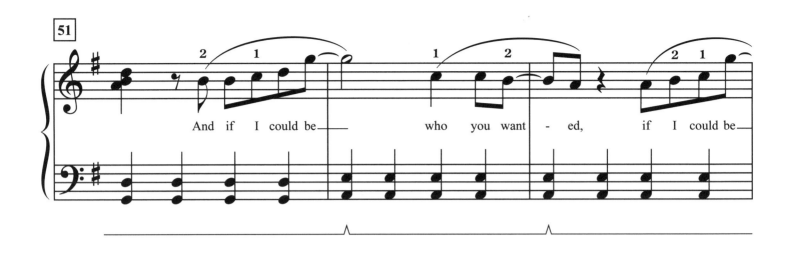

And if I could be_____ who you want - ed, if I could be_____

_____ who you want - ed, all_____ the time,

all_____ the time.

mp   *rit.*

I Don't Want to Miss a Thing

(from *Armageddon*)

Words and Music by Diane Warren
Arranged by Dan Coates

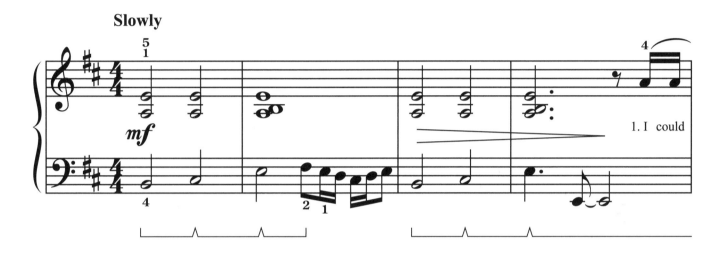

I'd Lie for You
(And That's the Truth)

Words and Music by Diane Warren
Arranged by Dan Coates

Moderately slow

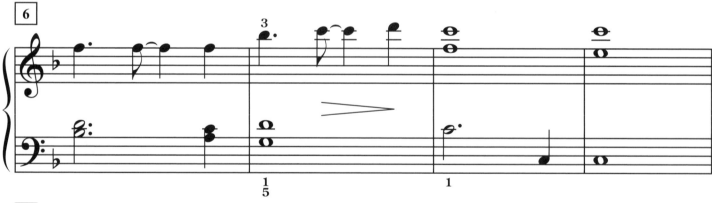

Verse:

1. I'd nev-er tell you one lie,___ I'd nev-er let you down. I'd nev-er leave, I'd be the
2. Just take a look in my eyes,___ you'll see a love that's blind. Just take a hold of my hand,

© 1995 REALSONGS (ASCAP)
All Rights Reserved

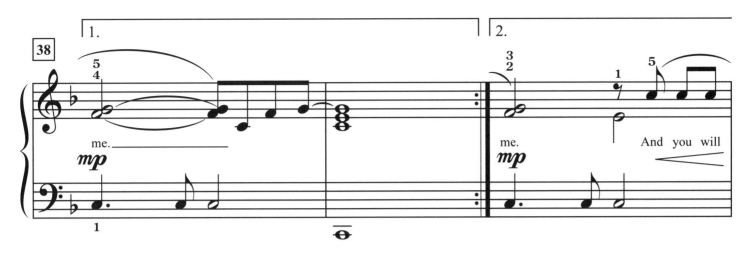

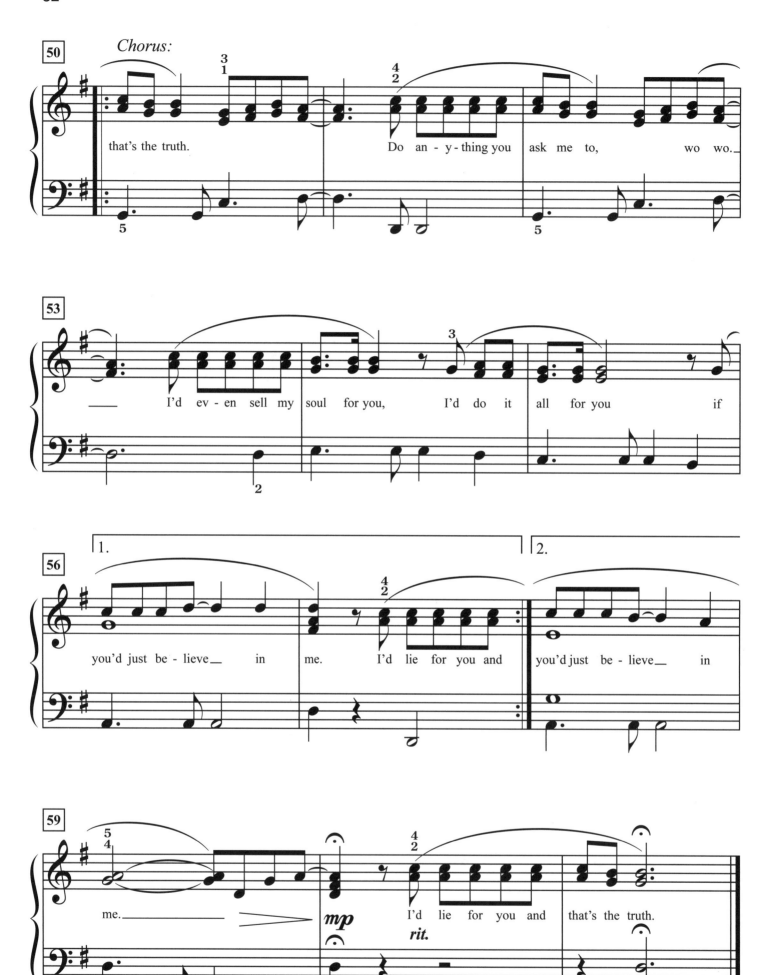

I'll Be There for You
(Theme from *Friends*)

Words by David Crane, Marta Kauffman,
Allee Willis, Phil Solem and Danny Wilde
Music by Michael Skloff
Arranged by Dan Coates

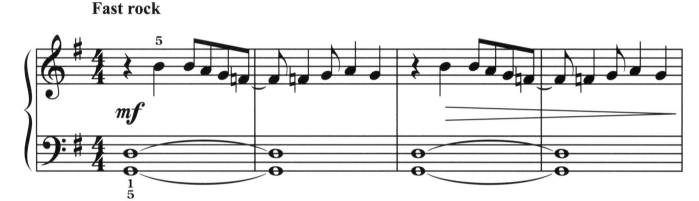

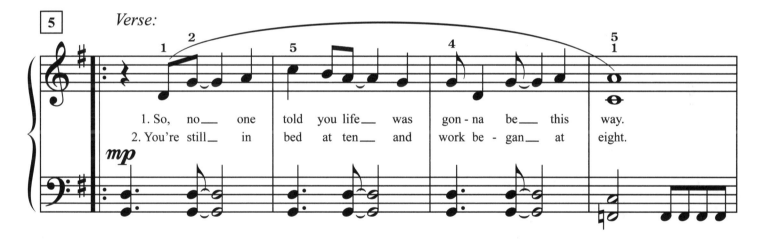

1. So, no__ one told you life__ was gon - na be__ this way.
2. You're still__ in bed at ten__ and work be - gan__ at eight.

Your job's__ a joke, you're broke,__ your love life's D. O. A.
You've burned__ your break - fast, so__ far, ev - 'ry - thing is great.

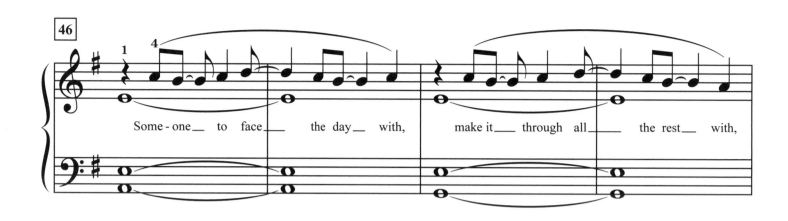

Some - one__ to face__ the day__ with, make it__ through all__ the rest__ with,

some - one I'll al - ways laugh with. E - ven at my worst,__ I'm best with

you._____

f

D.S. al Coda

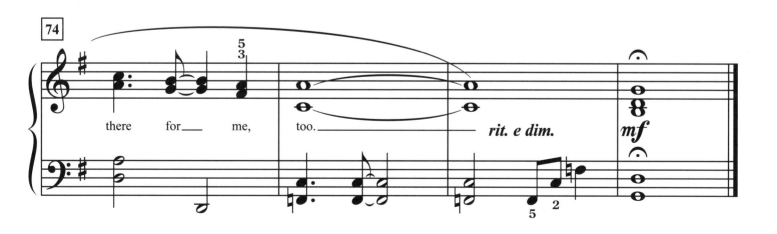

Losing My Religion

Words and Music by
William Berry, Peter Buck,
Michael Mills and Michael Stipe
Arranged by Dan Coates

Moderately, with steady rock beat

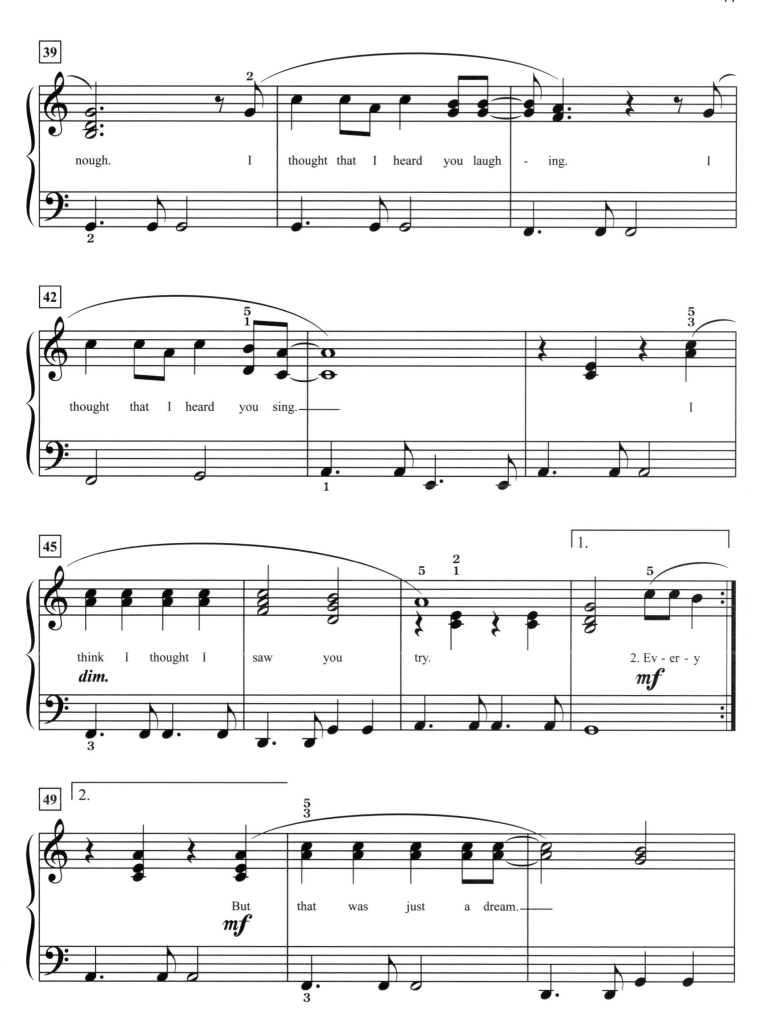

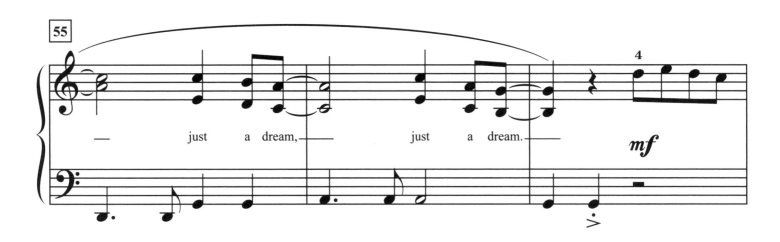

Verse 2:
Every whisper of every waking hour,
I'm choosing my confessions
Trying to keep an eye on you
Like a hurt, lost and blinded fool.
Oh no, I've said too much.
I set it up.
Consider this,
Consider this the hint of the century.
Consider this,
The slip that brought me to my knees failed.
What if all these fantasies come flailing around?
And now, I've said too much.
I thought that I heard you laughing.
I thought that I heard you sing.
I think I thought I saw you try.
(To Chorus:)

Love at First Sight

Words and Music by
Glen Burtnik, Dennis DeYoung and James Young
Arranged by Dan Coates

Moderately, with a steady beat

Macarena

Words and Music by
Antonio Romero and Rafael Ruiz
Arranged by Dan Coates

Moderately, with a dance beat

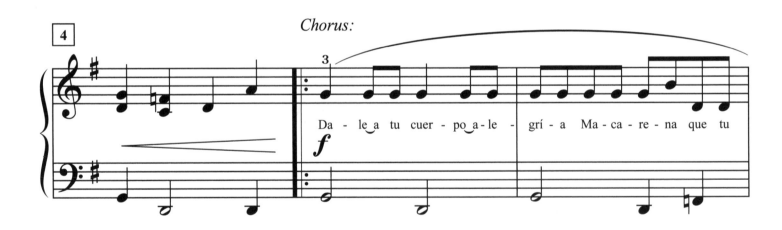

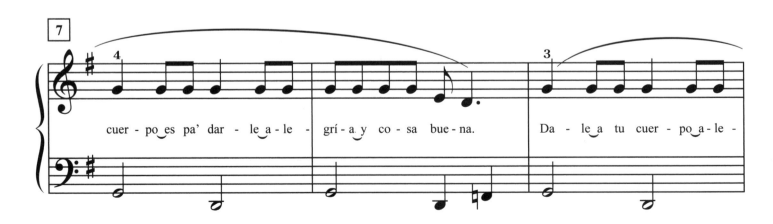

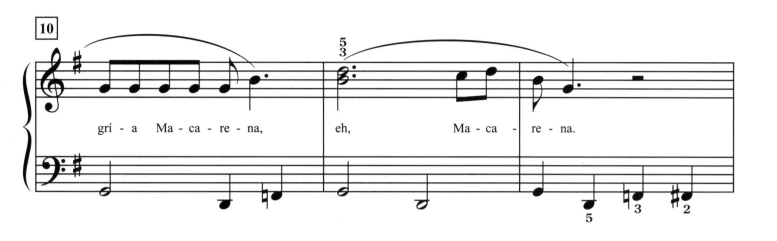

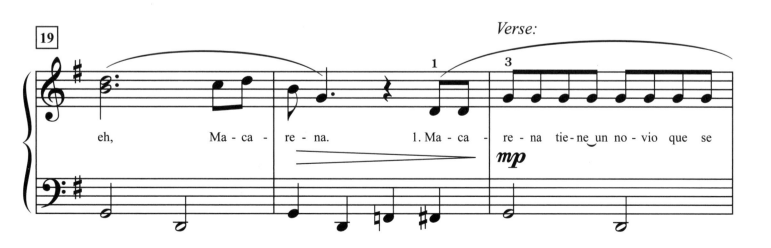

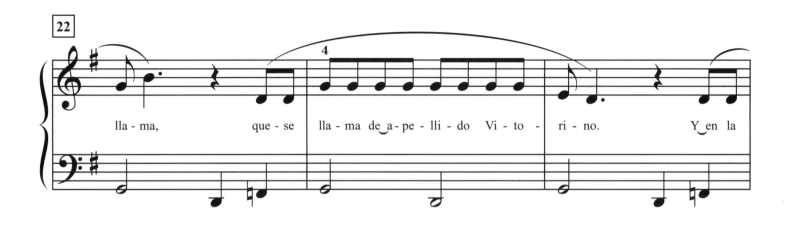

lla - ma, que - se lla - ma de a - pe - lli - do Vi - to - ri - no. Y en la

ju - ra de ban - de - ra del mu - cha - cho se la dió con dos a -

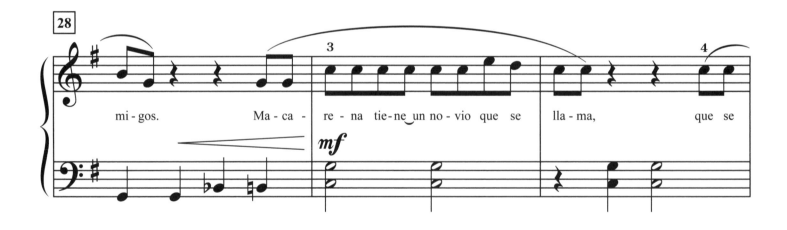

mi - gos. Ma - ca - re - na tie - ne un no - vio que se lla - ma, que se

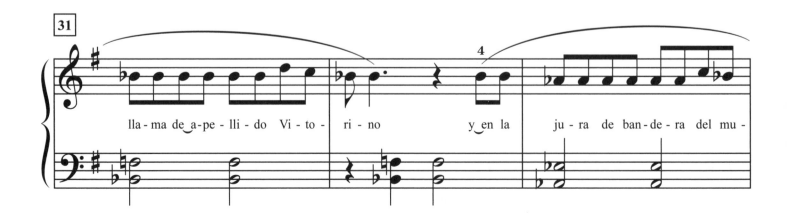

lla - ma de a - pe - lli - do Vi - to - ri - no y en la ju - ra de ban - de - ra del mu -

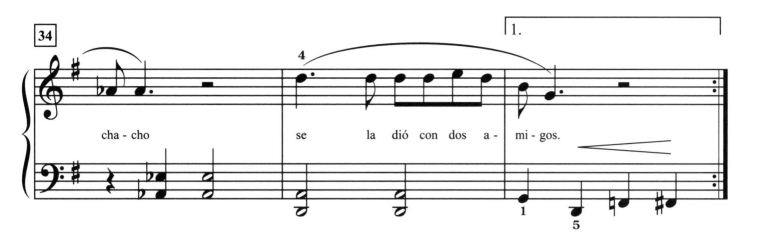

cha - cho se la dió con dos a - mi - gos.

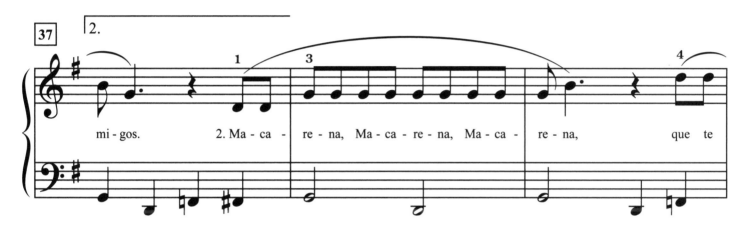

mi - gos. 2. Ma - ca - re - na, Ma - ca - re - na, Ma - ca - re - na, que te

gus - tan los ve - ra - nos de Mar - be - lla. Ma - ca - re - na, Ma - ca - re - na, Ma - ca -

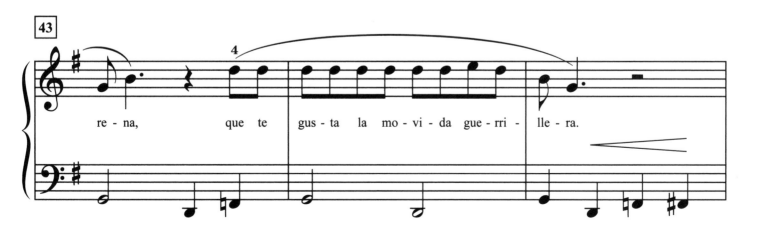

re - na, que te gus - ta la mo - vi - da gue - rri - lle - ra.

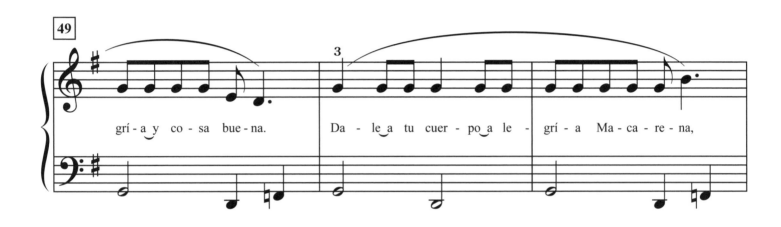

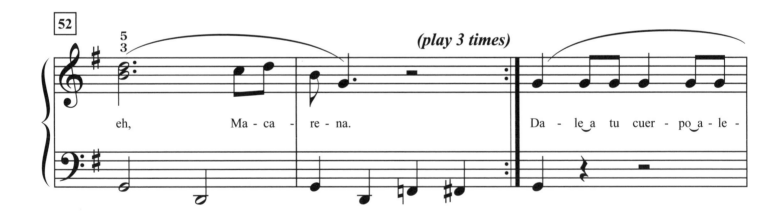

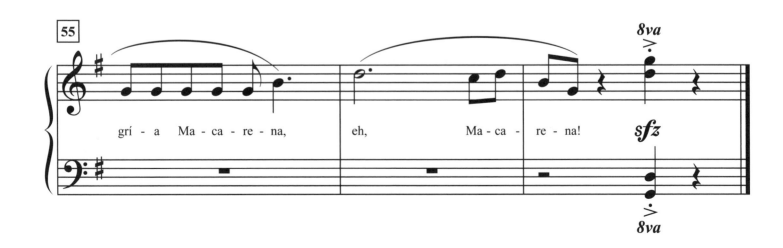

One of Us

Words and Music by Eric Bazilian
Arranged by Dan Coates

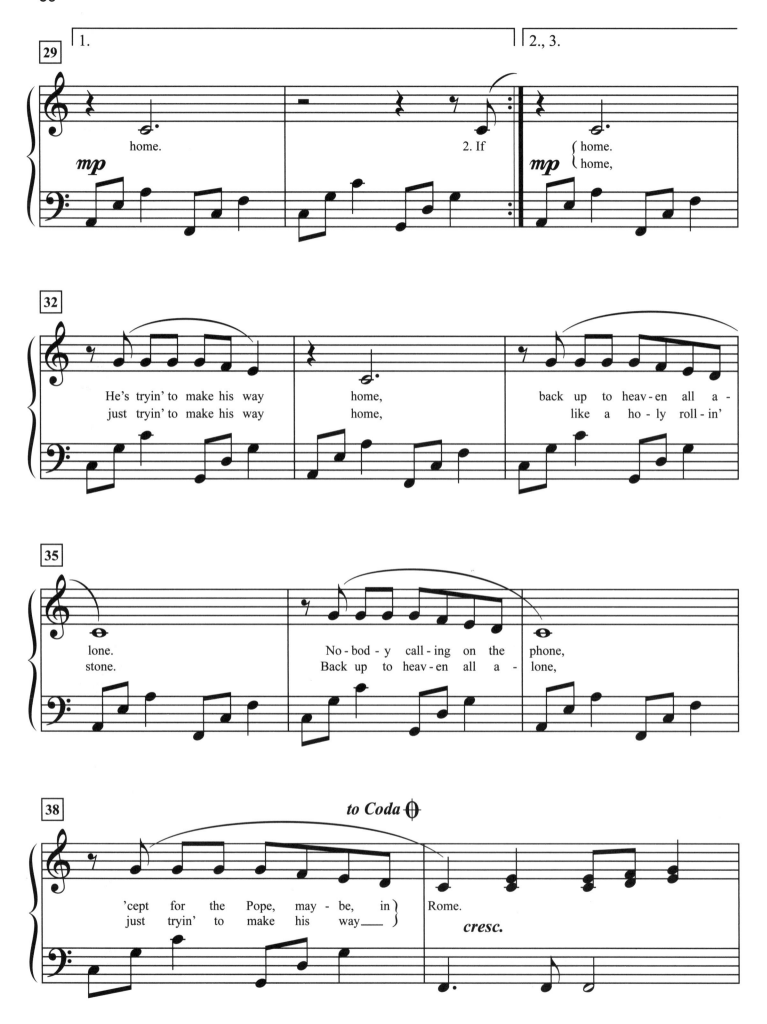

Right Now

Words and Music by
Sammy Hagar, Edward Van Halen,
Alex Van Halen and Michael Anthony
Arranged by Dan Coates

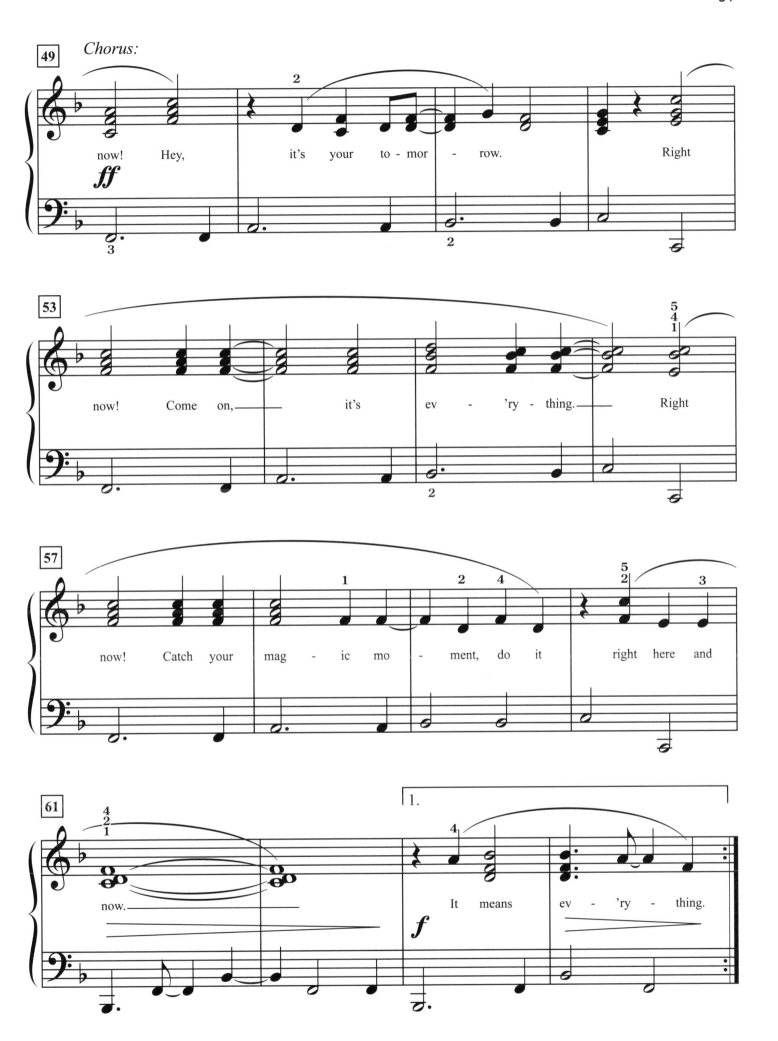

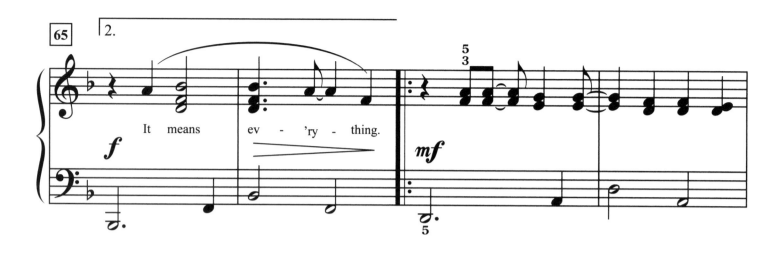

65 |2.

It means ev - 'ry - thing.

f   *mf*

69

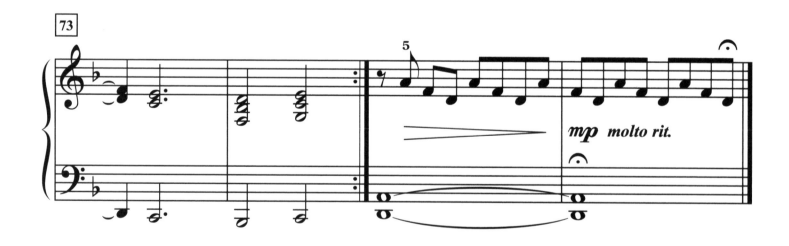

73

mp molto rit.

Verse 2:
Miss a beat, you lose the rhythm,
And nothing falls into place.
Only missed by a fraction,
Sent a little off your pace.
The more things you get, the more you want,
Just tradin' one for the other.
Workin' so hard to make it easy.
Got to turn, come on, turn this thing around.
(To Chorus:)

Streets of Philadelphia

Words and Music by
Bruce Springsteen
Arranged by Dan Coates

Moderately slow, with a steady beat

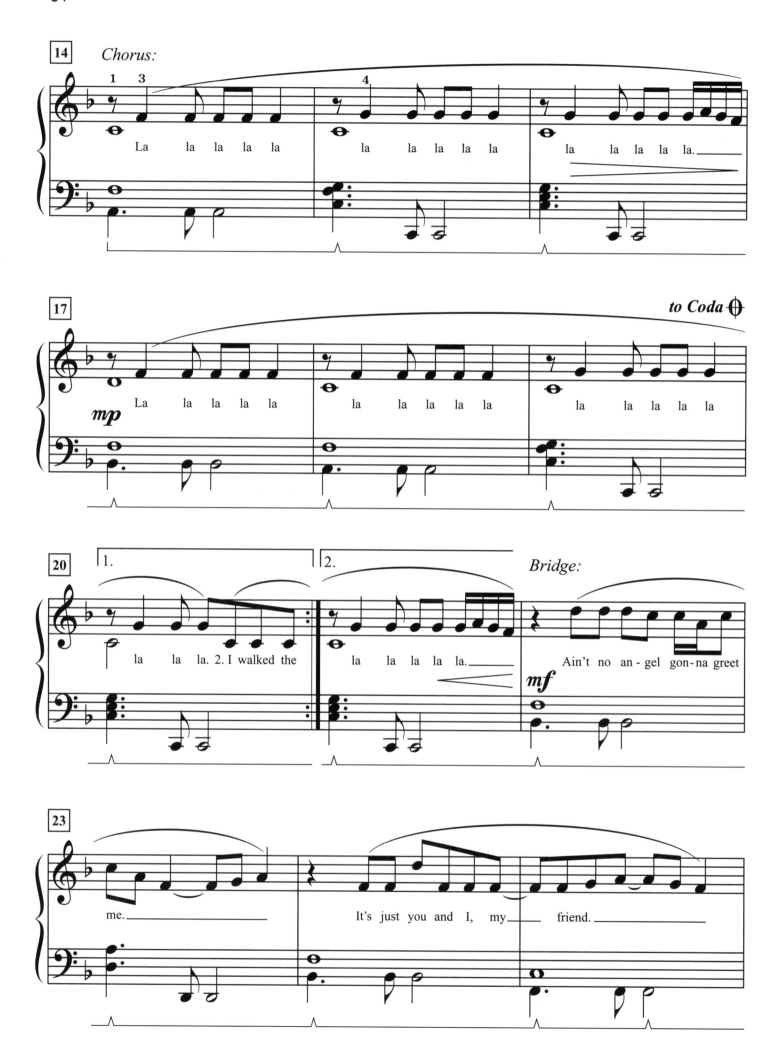

Verse 2:
I walked the avenue 'til my legs felt like stone.
I heard the voices of friends vanished and gone.
At night I could hear the blood in my veins
Just as black and whispering as the rain
On the streets of Philadelphia.
(*To Chorus:*)

Verse 3:
The night has fallen, I'm lyin' awake.
I can feel myself fading away.
So, receive me, brother, with your faithless kiss,
Or will we leave each other alone like this
On the streets of Philadelphia?
(*To Chorus:*)

Smooth

Words and Music by
Itaal Shur and Rob Thomas
Arranged by Dan Coates

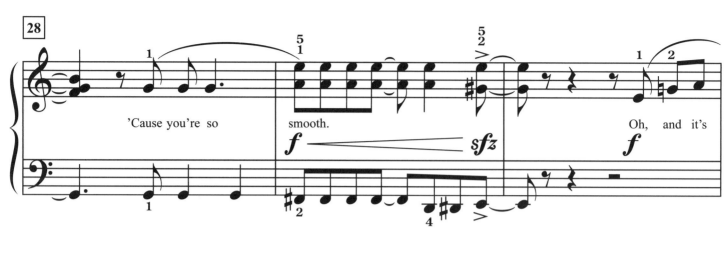

'Cause you're so smooth. Oh, and it's

Chorus:

just like the o - cean un - der the moon._ Well, it's the same as the e - mo - tion that I

get from you._____ You got the kind of lov - ing that can be so smooth,_ yeah.

Give me your heart,_ make it real, or else for - get a - bout it.

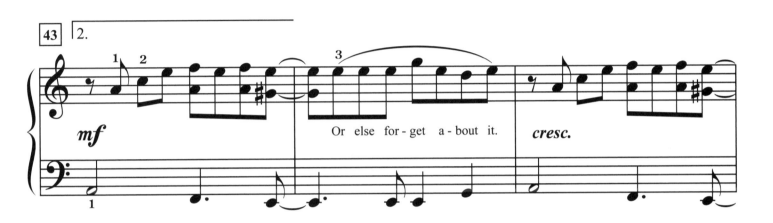

Verse 2:
Well, I'll tell you one thing,
If you should leave, it'd be a crying shame.
In every breath and every word
I hear your name calling me out, yeah.
Well, out from the barrio,
You hear my rhythm on your radio.
You feel the tugging of the world,
So soft and slow, turning you 'round and 'round.
And if you said this life ain't good enough,
I would give my world to lift you up.
I could change my life to better suit your mood.
'Cause you're so smooth.
(To Chorus:)

Walkin' on the Sun

Words and Music by
Steve Harwell, Gregory Camp,
Paul DeLisle and Kevin Iannello
Arranged by Dan Coates

ten, your neigh-bor-hood is un - der at -tack. Put a - way the crack be - fore the crack

puts you a - way.___ You need to be there when your ba-by's old e - nough to re - late.___

Chorus:

So don't de - lay, act now.___ Sup-plies are run - ning out.___ Al - low, if you're still a - live,

___ six to eight years to ar - rive.___ And if you fol-low, there may___ be a to-mor-row. But if___

Verse 2:
Twenty-five years ago they spoke out
And they broke out of recession and oppression.
And together they toked and they folked out with guitars
Around a bonfire, just singin' and clappin', man, what the hell happened?
Yeah, some were spellbound, some were hell bound,
Some, they fell down and some got back up and fought back against the meltdown.
And their kids were hippie chicks, all hypocrites
Because their fashion is smashin' the true meaning of it.
(To Chorus:)

What's the Frequency, Kenneth?

Words and Music by
William Berry, Peter Buck,
Michael Mills and Michael Stipe
Arranged by Dan Coates

Steady rock beat

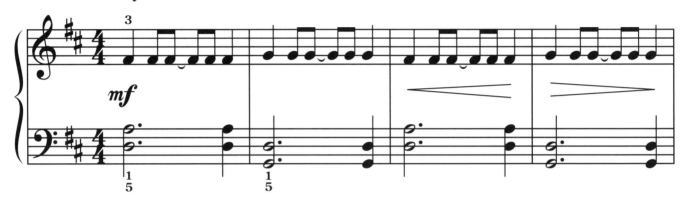

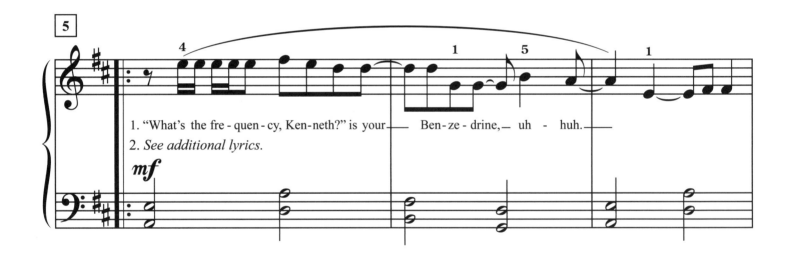

1. "What's the fre-quen-cy, Ken-neth?" is your Ben-ze-drine, uh - huh.
2. *See additional lyrics.*

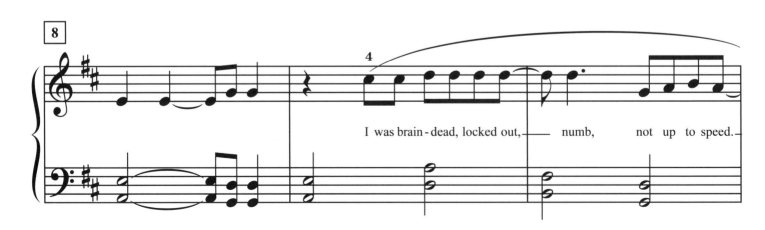

I was brain-dead, locked out, numb, not up to speed.

I thought I'd pegged you, an i-di-ot's dream.— Tun-nel vi-sion from the out-sid-er's screen.—

1.

I nev-er un-der-stood the fre-quen-cy,— uh - huh.—

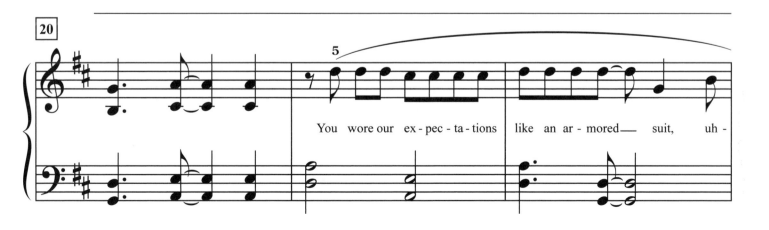

You wore our ex-pec-ta-tions like an ar-mored— suit, uh -

huh.

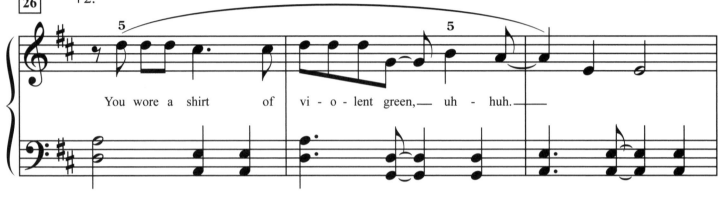

2.

You wore a shirt of vi - o - lent green, — uh - huh. —

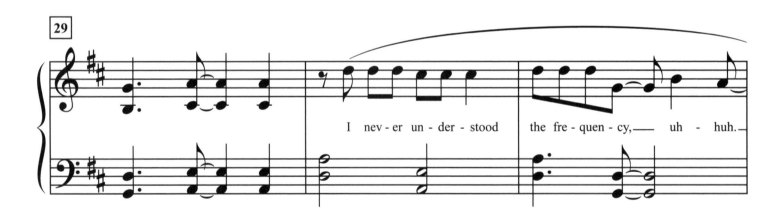

I nev - er un - der - stood the fre - quen - cy, — uh - huh.

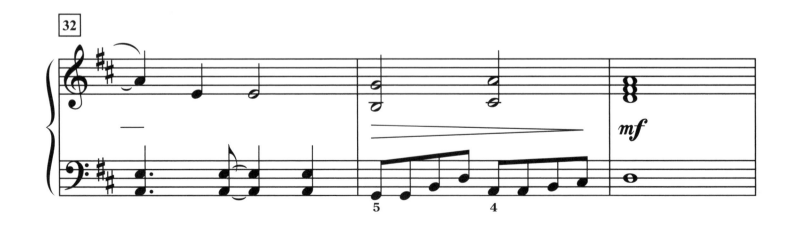

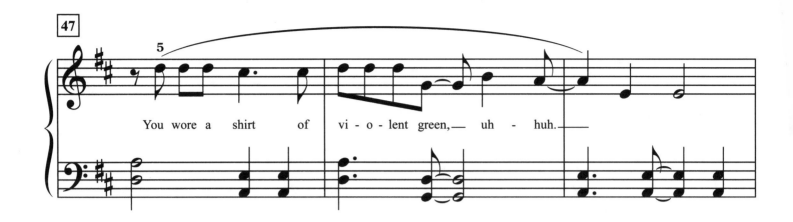

You wore a shirt of vi - o - lent green,— uh - huh.

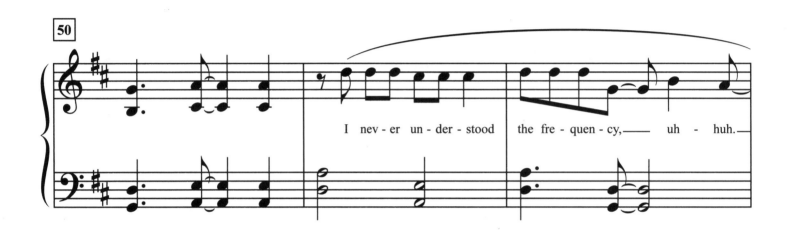

I nev - er un - der - stood the fre - quen - cy,— uh - huh.—

Verse 2:
I'd studied your cartoons, radio, music, T.V., movies, magazines.
Richard said, "Withdrawal in disgust is not the same as apathy."
You smile like the cartoon, tooth for a tooth,
You said that irony was the shackles of youth.
You wore a shirt of violent green, uh-huh.
I never understood the frequency, uh-huh.